Alfred's
**INSTRUMENTAL**
mp3 CD
**PLAY-ALONG**

# Ultimate Movie
## Instrumental Solos

Piano Solo
**THE PINK PANTHER**
Music by HENRY MANCINI

**OBLIVIATE**
Harry Potter

**THE NOTEBOOK**
COMPOSED BY AARON ZIGMAN

**ACROSS THE STARS**
(Love Theme from Star Wars : Episode II)
Music by JOHN WILLIAMS

**A WINDOW TO THE PAST
& DOUBLE TROUBLE**
HARRY POTTER AND THE PRISONER OF AZKABAN
Music by JOHN WILLIAMS

**Harry Potter**

**ROCKY BALBOA**
THE BEST OF ROCKY

**INDIANA JONES (Raiders March)**
by John Williams

**WONKA'S WELCOME SONG**

**Charlie** and the CHOCOLATE FACTORY

**Arranged by Bill Galliford, Ethan Neuburg, and Tod Edmondson
Recordings produced by Dan Warner, Doug Emery, Lee Levin and Artemis Music Limited.**

© 2012 Alfred Music Publishing Co., Inc.
All Rights Reserved. Printed in USA.

ISBN-10: 0-7390-9188-3
ISBN-13: 978-0-7390-9188-3

**Alfred**

# CONTENTS

# AUGIE'S GREAT MUNICIPAL BAND

(from *Star Wars Episode I: The Phantom Menace*)

Track 2: Demo
Track 3: Play-Along

Music by
JOHN WILLIAMS

# ACROSS THE STARS

(Love Theme from *Star Wars Episode II: Attack of the Clones*)

Track 4: Demo
Track 5: Play-Along

Music by
JOHN WILLIAMS

Across the Stars - 2 - 1

# ANAKIN'S THEME

## (from *Star Wars Episode I: The Phantom Menace*)

Music by
JOHN WILLIAMS

Track 6: Demo
Track 7: Play-Along

**Moderato** (♩ = 76)

*(Tempo click)*

Anakin's Theme - 2 - 1

# BATTLE OF THE HEROES
## (from *Star Wars Episode III: Revenge of the Sith*)

Track 8: Demo
Track 9: Play-Along

Music by
JOHN WILLIAMS

Battle of the Heroes - 2 - 1

# CAN YOU READ MY MIND?

(Love Theme from *Superman*)

Words by LESLIE BRICUSSE
Music by JOHN WILLIAMS

Track 10: Demo
Track 11: Play-Along

# CONCERNING HOBBITS

### (from *The Lord of the Rings: The Fellowship of the Ring*)

Track 12: Demo
Track 13: Play-Along

Music by
HOWARD SHORE

# CANTINA BAND

(from *Star Wars Episode IV: A New Hope*)

Track 14: Demo
Track 15: Play-Along

Music by
JOHN WILLIAMS

Moderately fast ragtime (♩ = 112)

*to measure* 57

*To Coda* ⊕

Cantina Band - 2 - 1

# DIAMONDS ARE FOREVER

Track 16: Demo
Track 17: Play-Along

Music by JOHN BARRY
Lyric by DON BLACK

# DOUBLE TROUBLE

(from *Harry Potter and the Prisoner of Azkaban*)

Music by
JOHN WILLIAMS

**Medieval in spirit** (♩ = 92)

# DING-DONG! THE WITCH IS DEAD

(from *The Wizard of Oz*)

Track 20: Demo
Track 21: Play-Along

Music by HAROLD ARLEN
Lyric by E.Y. HARBURG

Ding-Dong! The Witch Is Dead - 2 - 1

# DUEL OF THE FATES
## (from *Star Wars Episode I: The Phantom Menace*)

Track 22: Demo
Track 23: Play-Along

Music by
JOHN WILLIAMS

Duel of the Fates - 2 - 1

# EVENSTAR
## (from *The Lord of the Rings: The Two Towers*)

Music by HOWARD SHORE
Text by J.R.R. TOLKIEN

# FOLLOW THE YELLOW BRICK ROAD/ WE'RE OFF TO SEE THE WIZARD

(from *The Wizard of Oz*)

Track 26: Demo
Track 27: Play-Along

Music by HAROLD ARLEN
Lyric by E.Y. HARBURG

# FAMILY PORTRAIT
### (from *Harry Potter and the Sorcerer's Stone*)

Track 28: Demo
Track 29: Play-Along

Music by
JOHN WILLIAMS

**Slowly, with expression** ($\quad$ = 80)

\* An easier 8th-note alternative figure has been provided.

Family Portrait - 2 - 1

# FAWKES THE PHOENIX
### (from *Harry Potter and the Chamber of Secrets*)

Track 30: Demo
Track 31: Play-Along

Music by
JOHN WILLIAMS

Fawkes the Phoenix - 2 - 1

*An easier 8th-note alternative figure has been provided.

# FOR YOUR EYES ONLY

Track 32: Demo
Track 33: Play-Along

Music by BILL CONTI
Lyrics by MICHAEL LEESON

# FROM RUSSIA WITH LOVE

Track 34: Demo
Track 35: Play-Along

Words and Music by
LIONEL BART

# GOLDFINGER

Track 36: Demo
Track 37: Play-Along

Music by JOHN BARRY
Lyrics by LESLIE BRICUSSE
and ANTHONY NEWLEY

# HARRY'S WONDROUS WORLD

(from *Harry Potter and the Sorcerer's Stone*)

Track 38: Demo
Track 39: Play-Along

Music by
JOHN WILLIAMS

Harry's Wondrous World - 3 - 1

* E♯ = F

# GOLLUM'S SONG

(from *The Lord of the Rings: The Two Towers*)

Track 40: Demo
Track 41: Play-Along

Music by HOWARD SHORE
Words by FRAN WALSH

Moderately, flowing (♩ = 104)

Gollum's Song - 2 - 1

# GONNA FLY NOW

## (Theme from *Rocky*)

Words and Music by
BILL CONTI, AYN ROBBINS
and CAROL CONNORS

Track 42: Demo
Track 43: Play-Along

Gonna Fly Now - 2 - 1

# HEDWIG'S THEME

(from *Harry Potter and the Sorcerer's Stone*)

Music by
JOHN WILLIAMS

# I SWEAR

(from *The Social Network*)

Words and Music by
GARY BAKER and FRANK MYERS

# IF I ONLY HAD A BRAIN
## (from *The Wizard of Oz*)

Track 48: Demo
Track 49: Play-Along

Music by HAROLD ARLEN
Lyric by E.Y. HARBURG

# IN DREAMS

(from *The Lord of the Rings: The Fellowship of the Ring*)

Track 50: Demo
Track 51: Play-Along

Words and Music by
FRAN WALSH and
HOWARD SHORE

# JAMES BOND THEME

(from *Dr. No*)

By
MONTY NORMAN

Moderately bright (♩ = 138)

*With a slight swing feeling*

*(straight eighths)*

# LEAVING HOGWARTS
## (from *Harry Potter and the Sorcerer's Stone*)

Music by
JOHN WILLIAMS

Track 56: Demo
Track 57: Play-Along

# LILY'S THEME
## (Main Theme from *Harry Potter and the Deathly Hallows, Part 2*)

Music by
ALEXANDRE DESPLAT

Slowly, with expression (♩ = 72)

# MANY MEETINGS

### (from *The Lord of the Rings: The Fellowship of the Ring*)

Music by
HOWARD SHORE

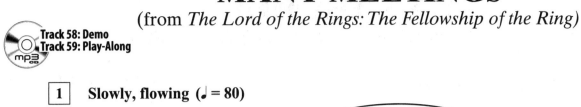

Track 58: Demo
Track 59: Play-Along

# LIVE AND LET DIE

Track 60: Demo
Track 61: Play-Along

Words and Music by
PAUL McCARTNEY and
LINDA McCARTNEY

Live and Let Die - 2 - 1

# MARION'S THEME

(from *Raiders of the Lost Ark*)

Track 62: Demo
Track 63: Play-Along

Music by
JOHN WILLIAMS

# MAY THE FORCE BE WITH YOU

(from *Star Wars Episode IV: A New Hope*)

Track 64: Demo
Track 65: Play-Along

Music by
JOHN WILLIAMS

# NOBODY DOES IT BETTER

(from *The Spy Who Loved Me*)

Track 66: Demo
Track 67: Play-Along

Music by MARVIN HAMLISCH
Lyrics by CAROLE BAYER SAGER

# OBLIVIATE
### (from *Harry Potter and the Deathly Hallows, Part 2*)

Track 68: Demo
Track 69: Play-Along

Music by
ALEXANDRE DESPLAT

# ON HER MAJESTY'S SECRET SERVICE

By JOHN BARRY

Track 72: Demo
Track 73: Play-Along

### (YOU'RE OUT OF THE WOODS)
# OPTIMISTIC VOICES
(from *The Wizard of Oz*)

Lyric by
E.Y. HARBURG

Music by
HAROLD ARLEN and
HERBERT STOTHART

**Moderately bright (♩ = 104)**

Track 74: Demo
Track 75: Play-Along

# OVER THE RAINBOW
(from *The Wizard of Oz*)

Lyric by
E.Y. HARBURG

Music by
HAROLD ARLEN

# PRINCESS LEIA'S THEME
### (from *Star Wars Episode IV: A New Hope*)

Music by
JOHN WILLIAMS

Moderately slow, with a gentle flow (♩ = 72)

# RAIDERS MARCH

(from *Raiders of the Lost Ark*)

Music by
JOHN WILLIAMS

Track 78: Demo
Track 79: Play-Along

March (♩ = 126)

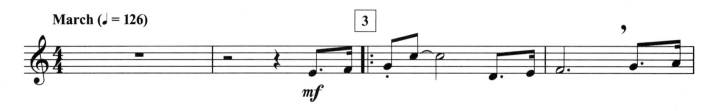

Raiders March - 2 - 1

Track 80: Demo
Track 81: Play-Along

# ROHAN
(from *The Lord of the Rings: The Two Towers*)

Text by
J.R.R. TOLKIEN

Music by
HOWARD SHORE

**Moderately (♩ = 76)**
(Tempo click)

**1** *EOWYN'S THEME*

**17** *THE KING OF THE GOLDEN HALL*

# SONG FROM M*A*S*H
## (Suicide Is Painless)

**Track 82: Demo**
**Track 83: Play-Along**

Words and Music by
MIKE ALTMAN and JOHNNY MANDEL

# STAR WARS
(Main Theme)
(from *Star Wars Episode IV: A New Hope*)

Track 84: Demo
Track 85: Play-Along

Music by
JOHN WILLIAMS

# STATUES

### (from *Harry Potter and the Deathly Hallows, Part 2*)

By
ALEXANDRE DESPLAT

Track 86: Demo
Track 87: Play-Along

**Moderately, with movement (♩ = 132)**

# THE STEWARD OF GONDOR

(from *The Lord of the Rings: The Return of the King*)

Track 88: Demo
Track 89: Play-Along

Lyrics by
J.R.R. TOLKIEN
Adapted by
PHILIPPA BOYENS

Music by
HOWARD SHORE
Contains the Composition "The Edge Of Night"
Melody by BILLY BOYD

# THE BLACK RIDER

(from *The Lord of the Rings: The Fellowship of the Ring*)

Music by
HOWARD SHORE

# THEME FROM SUPERMAN

Track 92: Demo
Track 93: Play-Along

Music by
JOHN WILLIAMS

Theme from Superman - 2 - 1

Theme from Superman - 2 - 2

# THE ARENA
### (from *Star Wars Episode II: Attack of the Clones*)

Track 94: Demo
Track 95: Play-Along

Music by
JOHN WILLIAMS

The Arena - 2 - 1

# THE IMPERIAL MARCH (DARTH VADER'S THEME)

### (from *Star Wars Episode V: The Empire Strikes Back*)

Music by
JOHN WILLIAMS

Track 96: Demo
Track 97: Play-Along

# THE LULLABY LEAGUE/
# THE LOLLIPOP GUILD/
# WE WELCOME YOU TO MUNCHKINLAND

*(from The Wizard of Oz)*

Track 98: Demo
Track 99: Play-Along

Music by HAROLD ARLEN
Lyric by E.Y. HARBURG

# THE MEADOW PICNIC

(from *Star Wars Episode II: Attack of the Clones*)

Track 100: Demo
Track 101: Play-Along

Music by
JOHN WILLIAMS

# THE MERRY OLD LAND OF OZ

(from *The Wizard of Oz*)

Track 102: Demo
Track 103: Play-Along

Music by HAROLD ARLEN
Lyric by E.Y. HARBURG

# THE NOTEBOOK
## (Main Title)

Written by
AARON ZIGMAN

Track 104: Demo
Track 105: Play-Along

# THE PROPHECY
### (from *The Lord of the Rings: The Fellowship of the Ring*)

Track 106: Demo
Track 107: Play-Along

Music by HOWARD SHORE
Text by J.R.R. TOLKIEN
Adapted by PHILLIPPA BOYENS

# THE PINK PANTHER

## (from *The Pink Panther*)

Track 108: Demo
Track 109: Play-Along

By HENRY MANCINI

Moderately, mysterious (♩ = 120)

**23** Swing

The Pink Panther - 2 - 1

# THE THRONE ROOM
## (from *Star Wars Episode IV: A New Hope*)

Track 110: Demo
Track 111: Play-Along

Music by
JOHN WILLIAMS

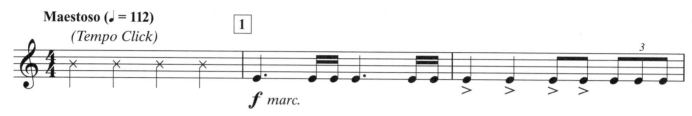

Maestoso (♩ = 112)
(Tempo Click)

*f* marc.

The Throne Room - 2 - 1

# THUNDERBALL
(Main Theme)

Music by JOHN BARRY
Lyric by DON BLACK

Track 112: Demo
Track 113: Play-Along

Moderately slow (♩ = 92)

# TOMORROW NEVER DIES

Track 114: Demo
Track 115: Play-Along

Words and Music by
SHERYL CROW and
MITCHELL FROOM

# WIZARD WHEEZES
## (from *Harry Potter and the Half-Blood Prince*)

Track 116: Demo
Track 117: Play-Along

Music by
NICHOLAS HOOPER

Wizard Wheezes - 2 - 1

# WONKA'S WELCOME SONG

## (from *Charlie and the Chocolate Factory*)

Track 118: Demo
Track 119: Play-Along

Words by JOHN AUGUST and DANNY ELFMAN
Music by DANNY ELFMAN

(À la yodel)

# YOU ONLY LIVE TWICE

Track 120: Demo
Track 121: Play-Along

Music by JOHN BARRY
Lyric by LESLIE BRICUSSE

# PARTS OF A CLARINET AND FINGERING CHART

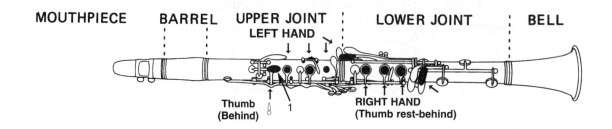

● = press the key or cover the hole with your finger.
○ = do not press the key or cover the hole.

When there is more than one fingering given for a note, use the first one unless the alternate fingering is suggested.

# World of WarCraft

## INSTRUMENTAL SOLOS

This instrumental series contains themes from Blizzard Entertainment's popular massively multiplayer online role-playing game and includes 4 pages of art from the World of Warcraft universe. The compatible arrangements are carefully edited for the Level 2–3 player, and include an accompaniment CD which features a demo track and play-along track. Titles: Lion's Pride • The Shaping of the World • Pig and Whistle • Slaughtered Lamb • Invincible • A Call to Arms • Gates of the Black Temple • Salty Sailor • Wrath of the Lich King • Garden of Life.

(00-36626) I Flute Book & CD I $12.99

(00-36629) I Clarinet Book & CD I $12.99

(00-36632) I Alto Sax Book & CD I $12.99

(00-36635) I Tenor Sax Book & CD I $12.99

(00-36638) I Trumpet Book & CD I $12.99

(00-36641) I Horn in F Book & CD I $12.99

(00-36644) I Trombone Book & CD I $12.99

(00-36647) I Piano Acc. Book & CD I $14.99

(00-36650) I Violin Book & CD I $16.99

(00-36653) I Viola Book & CD I $16.99

(00-36656) I Cello Book & CD I $16.99

# Harry Potter

## INSTRUMENTAL SOLOS

Play-along with the best-known themes from the Harry Potter film series! The compatible arrangements are carefully edited for the Level 2–3 player, and include an accompaniment CD which features a demo track and play-along track.

Titles: Double Trouble • Family Portrait • Farewell to Dobby • Fawkes the Phoenix • Fireworks • Harry in Winter • Harry's Wondrous World • Hedwig's Theme • Hogwarts' Hymn • Hogwarts' March • Leaving Hogwarts • Lily's Theme • Obliviate • Statues • A Window to the Past • Wizard Wheezes.

(00-39211) | Flute Book & CD | $12.99
(00-39214) | Clarinet Book & CD | $12.99
(00-39217) | Alto Sax Book & CD | $12.99
(00-39220) | Tenor Sax Book & CD | $12.99
(00-39223) | Trumpet Book & CD | $12.99
(00-39226) | Horn in F Book & CD | $12.99
(00-39229) | Trombone Book & CD | $12.99
(00-39232) | Piano Acc. Book & CD | $18.99
(00-39235) | Violin Book & CD | $18.99
(00-39238) | Viola Book & CD | $18.99
(00-39241) | Cello Book & CD | $18.99